WHAT REALLY IS A FISHER OF MEN?

JHINELLE THOMPSON

What Really is A Fisher of Men

What Really is A Fisher of Men

Copyright © 2025 by Jhinelle Thompson
All rights reserved.

No part of this book may be reproduced, distributed, transmitted, or stored in any form or by any means—electronic, mechanical, photocopying, recording, or otherwise—without prior written permission from the author, except for brief quotations used in reviews or scholarly works.

This book is intended for informational and inspirational purposes only. While every effort has been made to ensure the accuracy and integrity of the content, no guarantees are made regarding outcomes or results. The views expressed are those of the author and are not intended to replace professional, legal, financial, medical, or spiritual counsel.

Scripture quotations, if used, are taken from the New King James Version (NKJV), Amplified Bible (AMP), and King James Version (KJV), unless otherwise noted.

Cover design by Jhinelle Thompson.

Printed in the United States of America.
First Edition.

ISBN: 9798242011304

Table of Contents

Dedication

Chapter One: Casting the Line

Chapter Two: What is a Disciple?

Chapter Three: The Design of Discipleship

Chapter Four: Building on the Word of God

Chapter Five: Bible study methods

Chapter Six: Living Out Scripture

Chapter Seven: The Holy Spirit's Role in Discipleship

Chapter Eight: Obedience in the Process

Chapter Nine: The Weight of Who You Follow

Chapter Ten: Spiritual Growth and Maturity

Chapter Eleven: Evangelism and Discipleship

What Really is A Fisher of Men

Dedication

To my sister Danielle,

Thank you for leading me to the water and urging me to drink. Your unwavering faith, encouragement, and Christ-centered love have been a beacon in my life. Through your obedience, I found salvation, and now I have the privilege of guiding others to that same life-giving stream. You've shown me the essence of discipleship in words and how you live with a heart humbly postured to serve Christ. Your life has inspired me to walk this path, and I am forever grateful. Thank you for being my personal editor.

With love and gratitude,
Your Little Sister Jhinelle

To My Sister Quera,

Thank you for taking the time to read and help complete the edits on this book. I couldn't have finished it without your help.

With love,
Your Sister Jhinelle

To Bianca,

Thank you for your encouragement, for teaching me what gentleness looks like in its purest form, and for the title of this book!

With love,
Your Sister in Christ Jhinelle

Mission Statement:
To equip and empower believers with a deep understanding of discipleship, living out Christ's teachings daily, and actively leading others to Him.

Chapter One: Casting The Line
Foundation

The Christian faith is the belief in one God, who exists in three persons: God the Father, God the Son (Jesus Christ), and God the Holy Spirit. This foundational belief shapes our perspective on the world, ourselves, and our place in it. God created the universe, everything in it, and humanity was created in God's image but fell into sin through disobedience (Genesis 1:26-27, Romans 3:23). This sin separated humanity from God. Still, God, in His great love and mercy, provided a way for reconciliation through the death and resurrection of His Son, Jesus Christ. Jesus, fully God and fully man, lived a sinless life. He died on the cross as a sacrifice for my sins and yours, and rose again on the third day, defeating death and offering eternal life to all who believe in Him (John 3:16, Romans 5:8, 1 Corinthians 15:3-4).

This foundation is essential because it clarifies our identity, purpose, and eternal destiny. Without it, we define our own terms of life. Through this faith, we are connected to the very heart of God. Understanding this sets the stage for everything else we'll learn about who we are in Him.

Faith comes from hearing the word of God. It is demonstrated through the testimony of Jesus Christ and the documented journey of those mentioned in the scriptures. Christians are called to follow Christ's example, loving God with all their heart, soul, and mind, and loving others as they love themselves (Matthew 22:37-40). Through faith in Jesus Christ, believers receive forgiveness for their sins and the gift of the Holy Spirit, who empowers them to live in accordance with God's will (Ephesians 1:13-14, Galatians 5:22-23). However, there's a difference between simply identifying as a Christian and walking as a Kingdom citizen. Many wear the title "Christian," but Kingdom citizenship means living with intentionality under Christ's rule and reign, submitting daily to His Lordship, representing His values, and expanding His influence on earth. This distinction helps us shift from cultural Christianity to a deeper, purpose-driven relationship with our Heavenly Father. The Christian life involves ongoing transformation through sanctification, becoming more like Christ, and sharing the gospel to spread God's Kingdom (Romans 12:1-2, Matthew 28:19-20). Christians look forward to the return of Jesus Christ, who will establish His eternal Kingdom and bring justice and peace to the world (Revelation 21:1-4).

The Art of Fishing and Fishing for Men

The rhythmic dance of fishing is a communion between the waters and the seeker. With every cast of the line and every ripple in the stillness, there's an act unfolding of patience, persistence, and purpose. Fishing is more than what you see with your eyes; it's an art and a way of life.

People fish for many reasons. Some fish to eat, drawing life from the sea to nourish their families. Others fish for the thrill, the tug of the line a testament to unseen life. Then, some fish for peace, standing at the water's edge to listen as the water and wind whisper through the breeze and the waves. Fishing teaches us the value of waiting. It's a reminder that the most significant rewards often require stillness and patience.

What Really is A Fisher of Men

From the anticipation of a tug on the line that promises food for the body to the quiet lessons that nourish the heart, every catch tells a story of effort intertwined with grace. But what if fishing is more than an act of survival or sport? What if it is a calling, a metaphor for the spiritual work we are invited to undertake?

Jesus made this parallel clear when He called His disciples, saying, "Follow Me, and I will make you fishers of men"(Matthew 4:19, NKJV). **This wasn't just poetic language; it was a direct invitation to the mission of evangelism. Like casting a line, sharing the gospel requires patience, persistence, and faith. Not every cast results in a catch, but the obedience to continue casting is where the faith lies.**

And what is the catch? The "catch" in this is not for sport but for eternity. It is the soul that finds salvation, the heart that turns toward Christ, and the life forever changed by His grace. Every soul saved is a victory, a celebration in Heaven as Luke 15:10 (NKJV) reminds us: "Likewise, I say to you, there is joy in the presence of the angels of God over one sinner who repents." Just as the fisherman shows up day after day, sometimes catching nothing but always hoping, the believer must go out into the world casting the net of truth, love, and the gospel. It's not always flashy or immediate, but it's sacred work. Each soul is a treasure. Each moment of sharing Christ, whether received or not, is an act of love, obedience, and purpose. So while fishing feeds the body, evangelism feeds eternity. This connection between fishing and evangelism is vital. It is the believer's call to be faithful fishers not of fish, but of people. And in every testimony, every life changed, we are reminded: it's not about how many we catch, but that we keep casting, trusting the Lord for the harvest to bring in what only He can.

Being a fisher of men isn't limited to preaching, teaching, or creating Christian content. It's a lifestyle that reflects Christ's heart. It's about listening compassionately, serving selflessly, and living in a way that draws others to Christ through our actions and lives. When we embody His love, we become vessels of His light, inviting others to experience the life-changing power of the gospel. When we love deeply, we mirror God's heart. When we extend peace in chaos, joy in sorrow, kindness when it's undeserved, and patience in waiting, we reflect Jesus to a world hungry for hope.

Living this way is fishing for men; it's casting nets through compassion, reeling souls in with grace, and anchoring others in God's truth through faithfulness and gentleness.

To fulfill this call, we must embark on a pilgrimage of growth, guided by the teachings of Christ and empowered by the Holy Spirit. The Holy Spirit cultivates these fruits in us not overnight, but through daily surrender and obedience. As we grow in the Spirit, our lives will speak louder than any sermon could, becoming living testimonies of God's transformative power. So let us fish for men not only with words, but with lives saturated in the fruit of the Spirit, trusting that as we reflect His nature, God will draw others to Himself through our obedience.

Before we dig deeper
It's essential to understand the spiritual forces at work, both the enemy we face and the Helper we've been given.

Recognizing the presence of the enemy and learning to hear the Holy Spirit is essential to walking in freedom, truth, and power.

Who is the enemy?

The enemy is satan, also referred to as the devil, the accuser, or the father of lies (John 8:44 NKJV). He is a deceiver whose sole mission is to steal, kill, and destroy (John 10:10 NKJV).

What does he do?

He whispers lies, sows confusion, tempts, distracts, and discourages. He'll use fear, shame, insecurity, pride, and even good things like relationships, success, or religion to pull you away from God's truth.

When does he attack?

Often during your moments of weakness, exhaustion, isolation, or transition. He attacks when you are vulnerable or about to walk into something greater. You have a target on your back every second you're awake and actively pursuing Christ.

Why does he do this?

Because he hates what God loves, and God loves You. He wants to keep you from fulfilling your purpose, experiencing God's love, saving souls, and knowing your true identity in Christ.

How can you recognize him?

When thoughts go against the Word of God, thoughts of unworthiness, condemnation, fear, confusion, division, or destruction, they are not from God. Pay attention to the fruit: If something produces fear, anxiety, or chaos, it's not of the Holy Spirit (2 Timothy 1:7 NKJV). The enemy thrives in lies and silence. That's why exposing him is the first step to defeating him.

The Holy Spirit: Who He Is and How to Hear Him

Who is the Holy Spirit?

The Holy Spirit is the Spirit of God, your Comforter, Advocate, and Teacher. He is the Spirit of truth (John 16:13 NKJV). The Holy Spirit was sent after Jesus ascended into Heaven to dwell within every believer (John 14:26 NKJV).

How do you hear Him?

The Holy Spirit speaks gently, with truth and love. He convicts but never condemns. He brings peace, even when giving corrections. You can hear Him through the Word of God, a quiet nudge in your spirit, a whisper, through dreams, people, or divine interruptions.

How do you know it's Him?

His voice aligns with Scripture and always leads you toward faith, righteousness, peace, love, and truth. Galatians 5:22-23 (NKJV) shows you the fruit of the Spirit, and that fruit is how you know you are hearing from Him.

Why is the Holy Spirit so integral?

The Holy Spirit is our helper in all things (John 14:26 NKJV). He empowers us to live out our faith (Acts 1:8 NKJV). He dwelt inside of us. We need the Holy Spirit to live a Holy life (Romans 8:9 NKJV)

How do you know he is actively guiding you?

He leads you into truth (John 16:13 NKJV), He produces spiritual fruit in your life (Galatians 5:22-23 NKJV), and He gives inner witness and confirmation (Romans 8:16 NKJV).

Do you need any other guide?

NO, any other guide is a family spirit (demon).

The Holy Spirit teaches everything necessary for godly living. (1 John 2:27 NKJV). God's Spirit + God's Word are the believer's ultimate guide(Psalm 119:105 NKJV).

Give God a Try – A Call to Action

If you're reading this and something inside you is stirring, if you're tired of the enemy's lies, if you're hungry for more, if you want truth, love, and purpose, try God. He is near to all who call on Him (Psalm 145:18 NKJV). This is your moment. He's not waiting for you to be perfect. He's waiting for you to say yes.

The Sinner's Prayer

　If you're ready to give your life to Christ and walk in freedom, pray this prayer from your heart:
"Lord Jesus, I believe that You are the Son of God. I believe You died for my sins and rose again so I could have eternal life. I repent for my sins, I repent for pride, unforgiveness, idolatry, lying, stealing, and every sin that has been reigning in my life. I turn away from everything that's not of You. I invite You into my heart to be my Lord and Savior. Fill me with Your Holy Spirit. Teach me how to walk in Your truth. From this day forward, I am Yours. In Jesus' name, Amen."
Romans 10:9 (NKJV) says, "If you confess with your mouth that Jesus is Lord and believe in your heart that God has raised Him from the dead, you will be saved."

Chapter Two: What is a disciple?

A disciple is a devoted follower of Jesus Christ who strives to embody His teachings, character, and mission. The term derives from the Greek word mathētēs, which means "learner" or "student." Discipleship transcends intellectual learning; it involves transformation, spiritual growth, and active participation in spreading the Gospel.

A disciple is not just a follower and a believer in Jesus Christ. A disciple is a servant, a worshiper, and an ambassador of Christ, a person marked by sacrifice and surrender. Being a disciple means committing to learn from Jesus, live like Him, and share His message with the world. Discipleship is not just a title; it's an active, intentional relationship defined by obedience, faith, and transformation. As Jesus declared in Matthew 16:24 (NKJV), "If anyone desires to come after Me, let him deny himself, and take up his cross, and follow Me." A legitimate disciple surrenders their will to God, seeks to align their life with His teachings, and becomes a living reflection of His love and truth.

Discipleship invites us into a life marked by sacrifice, worship, reverence, and a deep, abiding relationship with the Father, Son, and Holy Spirit. It is a daily choice to grow in His likeness and glorify His name in all we do. As Jesus declared in Luke 14:27 (NKJV), "And whoever does not bear his cross and come after Me cannot be My disciple." Carrying your cross means letting go of personal desires, wants, passions, and comforts, and embracing your heavenly Father's will above your own. It's an invitation to exchange our plans for His purpose, trusting that His ways are always better.

The Apostle Paul further illustrates this commitment in Romans 12:1 (AMP): "Therefore I urge you, brothers and sisters, by the mercies of God, to present your bodies [dedicating all of yourselves, set apart] as a living sacrifice, holy and well-pleasing to God, which is your rational (logical, intelligent) act of worship." Discipleship requires offering every part of ourselves, our thoughts, desires, actions, and decisions as a living sacrifice. It's a life that declares, "Lord, use me for Your glory. Whatever you say, I will do it. Lord, make my heart obey You."

To fully surrender as a disciple is to let Christ reign supreme in our lives, to let the Lord of Lords reign in our hearts, actions, and emotions. Galatians 2:20 (KJV) states, "I am crucified with Christ: nevertheless I live; yet not I, but Christ liveth in me: and the life which I now live in the flesh I live by the faith of the Son of God, who loved me and gave himself for me." Jesus modeled surrender in the Garden of Gethsemane when He prayed, "Not my will, but thine, be done" (Luke 22:42, KJV). As His followers, we are called to adopt the same posture of humility, trusting in God's perfect plan for our lives.

Chapter 3: The Design of Discipleship

The design of discipleship is a transformative journey that goes far beyond instruction or intellectual knowledge. Discipleship is about becoming like Christ, not just in words but in action, attitude, and how we engage with the world around us. Disciples view the world from a biblical worldview, a perspective on life where the teachings of the Word of God shape their understanding of the world and human existence. The Bible tells us that the Word became flesh in John 1:14-15 (NKJV): "And the Word became flesh and dwelt among us, and we beheld His glory, the glory as of the only begotten of the Father, full of grace and truth. John bore witness to Him and cried out, saying, "This was He of whom I said, 'He who comes after me is preferred before me, for He was before me.' "

A biblical worldview shapes one's understanding of reality, human nature, purpose, morality, and destiny, as informed by scripture. It acknowledges God as the Creator of all things and holds that the Bible provides absolute truth, guidance, and answers to life's most profound questions (The bible is life's manual). Discipleship is a lifelong growth and transformation process involving every aspect of our lives. The design of discipleship is to shape us into the image of Christ, cultivating in us the humility, character, boldness, love, and commitment to truth that He exemplified during His earthly ministry.

Discipleship requires intimate communion with Christ. It's about more than attending church services or memorizing scriptures. It's about living in a constant relationship with Him, seeking His guidance, listening to the voice of The Holy Spirit, and aligning our hearts, emotions, desires, and plans with His. This intimate relationship is not a passive experience; it demands active participation on our part. It involves a daily surrender to God, an openness to be shaped by His Word, consistent repentance, and a willingness to allow the Holy Spirit to mold our character.

In Luke 9:23, Jesus says, "Whoever wants to be my disciple must deny themselves and take up their cross daily and follow me." This scripture highlights the cost of discipleship, which involves self-denial and sacrifice. The discipleship design requires us to willingly surrender our desires, comforts, past lives, and ambitions to follow Jesus. It calls us to a life of sacrifice, where we prioritize God's will over our own. Discipleship is not just about personal gain; it's about aligning our lives with the mission of Christ to love, serve, and reach others with His message of hope. Discipleship is not meant to be a solitary or distant pursuit. The design of discipleship emphasizes the need for relational proximity. It's not enough to observe from afar or live in isolation. True discipleship requires intentional relationships and authentic connections with others on the same journey. Just as Jesus didn't remain distant or detached from His disciples, we are called to walk closely with one another in mutual support, accountability, and encouragement.

The "hand-over-hand" teaching method, as seen in Jesus' interactions with His disciples, is a powerful illustration of this relational design. Hand-over-hand guidance is a gentle, intentional method where the teacher places their hand over the learner's, guiding them step by step until the movement becomes their own. It's used when understanding hasn't yet formed, when hesitation holds them back, or when a steady hand is needed to shape the right action.

He didn't just give orders from a distance; He came alongside His followers, living with them and sharing their triumphs and trials. He demonstrated servant leadership, showing that true discipleship is not about power or status but service married to humility. By walking alongside His disciples, He modeled for us what it means to invest in the lives of others, to be present in their journey, and to guide them through life's challenges. This same principle applies to the power of community in the body of Christ. Spiritual growth is not a solo pursuit; it occurs most effectively within a healthy community. God has uniquely gifted each of us for a purpose within the body. As Paul writes in Romans 12:4-6 (NKJV), "For as we have many members in one body, but all the members do not have the same function, so we, being many, are one body in Christ, and individually members of one another. Having then gifts differing according to the grace that is given to us, let us use them: if prophecy, let us prophesy in proportion to our faith;" Some are gifted to teach, others to encourage, to lead, to serve, or to show mercy. No one is created to function alone.

Think of it like the human body: your heart, brain, lungs, and blood vessels all serve different roles, yet they depend on one another to keep you alive and well. Likewise, in the body of Christ, each member is essential. The church can't thrive if parts are missing or disconnected. It's just like a fisherman, he can't fish without his pole, the water, the bait, or the fish he wants to catch. It's a system where everything works together to fulfill a purpose.

In the same way, we need each other. We grow stronger, wiser, and more effective when we walk in unity, honoring the unique contributions of each person.

For example, 1 Corinthians 12:18-20 (NKJV) states, " But now God has set the members, each of them, in the body just as He pleased. And if they were all one member, where would the body be? But now indeed there are many members, yet one body." **So honor your part, honor others, and lean into community because it's in walking together that we reflect the fullness of Christ and grow into maturity.**

As disciples of Christ, we are called not only to follow His example but also to be agents of transformation in the lives of others. The design of discipleship extends beyond personal growth to include the responsibility of making disciples ourselves. In Matthew 28:19-20, Jesus gives His followers the Great Commission: "Therefore go and make disciples of all nations, baptizing them in the name of the Father and of the Son and of the Holy Spirit, and teaching them to obey everything I have commanded you." Discipleship is a cycle that begins with Jesus calling us to follow Him, and as we grow in Him, we are called to lead others on that same journey.

It is the ongoing process of being shaped into the likeness of Christ. It's not always easy or comfortable, but it is worth it. The discipleship design calls us to live intentionally, invest in relationships, and embrace a life of service, surrender, and growth. Through it all, we are reminded that our ultimate purpose is to reflect the love, grace, and truth of Jesus to a world that is desperately in need of His presence.

Themes I Noticed in My Discipleship Process
One of the most defining patterns I noticed in my discipleship journey was the rhythm of highs and lows, the constant tension between spiritual fire and spiritual fatigue. There were seasons I felt consumed by His presence, and others where I

wondered if I'd ever feel close to God again. Every time I pressed deeper into Him through prayer, fasting, or studying His Word, it seemed the intensity of spiritual warfare increased. Just as I began to ascend to new levels, the enemy pushed back with greater force.

Another battle I faced was spiritual dryness, those moments when my zeal for Scripture dimmed, and prayer felt more like warfare than worship. Yet, I learned that faithfully pursuing God, even in seasons of weariness, always bears fruit. "And let us not grow weary while doing good, for in due season we shall reap if we do not lose heart." (Galatians 6:9, NKJV).

There were also emotional sacrifices in walking away from people and places I deeply loved. That part of discipleship cost me dearly. But God began to teach me that loving Him must outweigh every other attachment. "He who loves father or mother more than Me is not worthy of Me. And he who loves son or daughter more than Me is not worthy of Me."(Matthew 10:37, NKJV). Choosing Him meant surrendering comfort, relationships, and my own will. I realized nothing compares to obedience. "For what will it profit a man if he gains the whole world, and loses his own soul?" (Mark 8:36, NKJV).

I also wrestled with deep feelings of unworthiness. I didn't believe I was capable of carrying the cross God placed before me. I felt too broken, too flawed, too far gone. I questioned why God would ever want to use me. I believed the lie that my voice held no weight, that my past disqualified me, that grace had somehow run out. I struggled to find authentic community, often feeling that many within the church were more devoted to tradition than to truth. I encountered performance, legalism, and a lack of sincerity, yet through it all, I kept pressing. **I kept showing up. I kept praying, even through tears. I kept fighting. I kept following Jesus.**

And you know what? **Jesus kept extending His hand. Each time I faltered, He lifted me higher. He kept reminding me that His love was steadfast, not conditional.** "The Lord has appeared of old to me, saying: 'Yes, I have loved you with an everlasting love; therefore, with lovingkindness I have drawn you.'" (Jeremiah 31:3, NKJV). He didn't leave me in my brokenness; He loved me into healing.

That is the beauty of discipleship: God doesn't just call you out of something; He walks you through it.

Be Encouraged

So if you're reading this and you're at the starting line, be encouraged. This walk isn't about perfection. It's about being willing. And if you've felt the nudge, if you're feeling drawn, it's because God has chosen you. "You have not chosen Me, but I have chosen you, and I have appointed and placed and purposefully planted you, so that you would go and bear fruit and keep on bearing, and that your fruit will remain and be lasting, so that whatever you ask of the Father in My name [as My representative] He may give to you." (John 15:16 AMP). It's not by chance. It's a divine appointment.

The process will be tedious. It will stretch you. There will be days when it feels like nothing's happening, but the Holy Spirit is always working. "I am convinced and confident of this very thing, that He who has begun a good work in you will [continue to] perfect and complete it until the day of Christ Jesus [the time of His return]."(Philippians 1:6 AMP). Don't get overwhelmed; rest in Christ. You are not just someone who attends church; you are a child of God, adopted into His family, with full access to His promises. "The Spirit you received brought about your adoption to sonship. And by him we cry, 'Abba, Father.'... Now if we are children, then we are heirs heirs of God and co-heirs with Christ" (Romans 8:15-17). **You already belong.** And everything I'm talking about here is obtainable, not by your strength, but by your surrender.

Different Types of Discipleship in My Life

My discipleship journey began when I witnessed my sister, Danielle, surrender her life fully to Jesus and become a woman radiant with wisdom, compassion, and grace. Her transformation revealed to me that God doesn't merely refine behavior; He renews the heart. Through her, I saw what it truly means for Christ to reshape a life from the inside out. Then came Pastor Hendricks, a living example of love in motion. He didn't just preach about love; he embodied it. I still remember how he invited my family complete strangers, to dinner simply to listen, to care, and to offer support. Yet his kindness extended far beyond that moment. When my younger sister was battling a rare form of leukemia, he stood beside us in prayer and presence, offering unwavering strength. Even when we drifted from the church, he never drifted from us. That is love lived out. Next came Pastor Jay, who taught me the power of spiritual warfare. She didn't merely speak about prayer; she demonstrated what it meant to intercede with authority, passion, and purpose. From her, I learned resilience, spiritual discipline, and what it means to stand firm in the presence of God.

Through every mentor, it was the Holy Spirit who became my most intimate teacher. He whispered correction when I strayed, stirred conviction when my heart grew cold, and spoke peace when the storms raged within me. When I forgot who I was, His gentle voice reminded me of whose I was. That still, steady presence has become my anchor. Through every mountain and valley, one truth has remained unshakable: discipleship cannot be built upon emotion or experience alone; it must be rooted in the living Word of God. People may plant seeds and others may water, but true growth, lasting, eternal growth, only comes when your life and discipleship are established on the Word of God.

Chapter Four: Building Discipleship on the Word of God

The Word of God is an invaluable tool, a blueprint that frames creation and guides us in every aspect of life. As 2 Timothy 3:16-17 (NKJV) declares: "All Scripture is given by inspiration of God and is profitable for doctrine, for reproof, for correction, for instruction in righteousness, that the man of God may be complete, thoroughly equipped for every good work." The Bible is the breath of God and spiritual food for man, infusing life and purpose into every believer. Being a true disciple of Jesus Christ without grounding oneself in His Word is impossible. The Scriptures serve as our instruction manual and spiritual food, revealing the heart of God and equipping us to live a life of holiness and righteousness.

The Word of God is the foundation of the discipleship journey. Without it, we cannot effectively follow Christ or disciple others. Through Scripture, we understand His will, learn His teachings, and are transformed by His truth. Psalm 119:105 (NKJV) affirms: "Your word is a lamp to my feet and a light to my path." The Bible guides us through life's complexities and challenges, illuminating our way. To be a disciple means to study God's Word and live it out daily. Living out the Word of God looks like embodying His attributes: showing kindness (Ephesians 4:32), walking in peace (Colossians 3:15), embracing patience (Galatians 5:22), forgiving others (Matthew 6:14-15), and pursuing His purpose (Jeremiah 29:11). It means transforming our knowledge of Scripture into actions that glorify God, allowing His truth to shine through our lives as a witness to the world.

Discipleship begins and thrives with the Word of God, our unshakable foundation and the source of life and light.

As disciples, how do we study and apply the Word of God effectively? Many believers struggle with prioritizing Scripture, often treating it as a secondary consideration rather than the central focus of their lives. Some may feel overwhelmed when reading the Bible, tired, distracted, or confused by its language, names, and meanings. You're not alone in this struggle. But the key is inviting the Holy Spirit into your study. Before diving into Scripture, prepare your heart with worship and praise. John 4:23 (AMP) states: But a time is coming and is already here when the true worshipers will worship the Father in spirit [from the heart, the inner self] and in truth; for the Father seeks such people to be His worshipers. Follow this with prayer, asking God for wisdom and understanding. Call on the Holy Spirit to guide you as you read.

Chapter Five: Bible study methods

There are many Bible study methods utilized to help you study scripture. Bible study methods refer to structured approaches used to study, interpret, and apply the Bible. These methods help readers engage with Scripture in a meaningful way, allowing them to gain a deeper understanding and personal insights.

<u>Prayer before reading</u>

Thank you, Heavenly Father, for all you do and who you are. Thank you for your wisdom, knowledge, and understanding. Forgive me for all my sins, all the known and unknown. Forgive me for exalting myself and my expertise above you. You are the Lord of Lords, the King of Kings, and Father, I need you. Lord, I need your help. I can not understand your words without you. There is nothing in this world that I could do without you. I surrender my mind, thoughts, emotions, and understanding to your Holy Spirit. Give me wisdom, knowledge, and understanding, and allow me to receive your word as you see fit. Allow me to see You in Your text. In Jesus' name, Amen.

What Really is A Fisher of Men

Bible Study Methods

Inductive Bible Study	Topical Bible Study	Book Study	Character Quality Study
• Observation: Begin by carefully observing the text. What does it say? Pay attention to key details, repeated words, themes, or patterns that recur throughout the text. • Interpretation: Ask questions about the meaning of the text. What does it mean? Consider the historical and cultural context, and examine the meanings of the words. • Application: Reflect on how the text applies to your life. How should it change your thinking, behavior, or beliefs? Seek to apply the lessons to daily living.	• Focus on a particular topic or theme in the Bible, such as "faith," "prayer," or "God's love." • Gather and study all related verses or passages across different books of the Bible. • Synthesize the information to gain a deeper understanding of the Bible's teachings on that topic.	• Choose a specific book or chapter of the Bible and study it in depth over time. • Break down the chapters or sections, explore background information about the author, audience, and purpose, and analyze the main points. • Reflect on the chapter's or book's overall message and how it fits into the larger biblical narrative.	• Choose a character quality, such as humility, patience, or kindness. • Identify verses and stories that illustrate this quality in biblical characters. • Explore how God develops this quality in people and reflect on your growth in this area.
Word Study	**Biographical Bible Study**	**Devotional Bible Study**	**Verse-by-Verse Study**
• Focus on a specific word or phrase in the Bible. • Look up the original Hebrew or Greek meaning, usage across different parts of the Bible, and variations in translation. • Explore the theological significance of the word and its implications.	• Study the life and character of a specific biblical figure, such as Moses, David, Ruth, or Paul. • Focus on that person's key events, decisions, and character traits, and see how God worked through them. • Apply lessons from their life to your walk.	• Approach Scripture to deepen your relationship with God. • Read smaller portions of Scripture and reflect on their significance, meditating on how God speaks to you through His word. • Focus on prayer and personal application.	• Carefully study each verse of a passage in a sequential manner, analyzing its meaning, context, and implications. • Use commentaries, concordances, and other study tools to dig deeper into each verse. • This method allows for a thorough and detailed understanding of Scripture.
Theological Bible Study	**Cross-Reference Study**	**SOAP Method**	**Verse Mapping**
• Study Scripture passages to gain a deeper understanding of specific theological doctrines, such as the Trinity, salvation, and eschatology. • Look for consistent teaching on these topics across the Bible and in various contexts. • Focus on deepening your understanding of God's nature and His plan for humanity.	• Use a Bible with cross-references to trace related verses throughout Scripture. • Look for connections between Old and New Testament passages, themes, prophecies, and fulfillments. • This method highlights the unity and continuity of the Bible's message.	• Scripture: Write down a verse or passage that stands out to you. • Observation: Record what you notice in the verse. What is God saying to you? • Application: Reflect on how this Scripture applies to your life. • Prayer: Pray to God about what you've learned and ask for His help in applying the lesson.	• Select and break a verse by studying keywords, phrases, and cross-references. • Look up the meanings of the original language, the historical context, and the related verses. • Create visual charts or notes that connect different aspects of the verse to facilitate a deeper understanding.

Chapter Six: Living Out Scripture

Living out Scripture isn't something you can do in your own strength; it requires full dependence on God the Father, the Holy Spirit, and Jesus Christ. True transformation begins when we learn to abide under the shadow of the almighty God. Jesus said in John 15:5 (NKJV), "I am the vine, you are the branches. He who abides in Me, and I in him, bears much fruit; for without Me you can do nothing."Without abiding in Him, we can't produce lasting fruit or walk in the calling placed on our lives. Living God's Word means taking it beyond reading or quoting it; it's about application. It means we allow the Word to shape our decisions, thoughts, and actions. Obedience becomes our response, not out of legalism, but out of love. James 1:22 (AMP) says, But prove yourselves doers of the word [actively and continually obeying God's precepts], and not merely listeners [who hear the word but fail to internalize its meaning], deluding yourselves [by unsound reasoning contrary to the truth]." Walking in the Word is a daily choice. When Scripture tells us what to lay down or pick up, we obey not selectively, but wholeheartedly.

For example, John 15:12 (AMP) states, "This is My commandment, that you love *and* unselfishly seek the best for one another, just as I have loved you." This love isn't convenient or conditional; it's sacrificial. It calls us to forgive even when it's difficult. **Forgiveness doesn't mean you have to restore every relationship, but it does mean releasing resentment and choosing mercy. That's how Christ loves us. He forgave us while we were still broken and rebellious.**

Romans 5:8 (AMP) reminds us, " But God clearly shows *and* proves His own love for us, by the fact that while we were still sinners, Christ died for us."

When you live the Word out loud, you don't just grow, you begin to Fish for Men. Every act of obedience is a cast of the net. Whenever you show love instead of hate, speak truth in love, or extend forgiveness, you become a vessel through which others encounter Christ. The ultimate goal of discipleship and spiritual maturity is not just personal growth; it's to give God glory and live out your divine purpose in abundance. Jesus said in John 10:10 (NKJV), "I have come that they may have life, and that they may have it more abundantly." That abundant life includes walking boldly in your assignment and leading others into theirs.

"It's the love of God that encourages us along the way to know that He knows best. Faith full-grown is belief, and belief full-grown is trust." - Danielle Thompson.

As Danielle Thompson put it, "It's the love of God that encourages us along the way to know that He knows best. Faith full-grown is belief, and belief full-grown is trust." And it's that kind of trust that produces endurance. Growth is not always loud or visible, but the Holy Spirit is always working, even in silence.

So, if you feel overwhelmed, take heart. You don't have to figure it all out. If you've been drawn to this walk, God chose you. John 15:16 (AMP) says, "You didn't choose me, remember; I chose you, and put you in the world to bear fruit, fruit that won't spoil. As fruit bearers, whatever you ask the Father in relation to me, he gives you." Your identity in Christ is secure. You're not wandering, you're walking as a child of God, fully loved and equipped.

Romans 8:15-17 (NKJV) says, "For you did not receive the spirit of bondage again to fear, but you received the Spirit of adoption by whom we cry out, 'Abba, Father.' The Spirit Himself bears witness with our spirit that we are children of God, and if children, then heirs of God and joint heirs with Christ." That's your identity. That's your inheritance. That's the confidence you walk in. So walk it out. Live the Word. Cast your net and step into your calling as a fisher.

Chapter Seven: The Holy Spirit's Role in Discipleship

The Holy Spirit plays a vital and multifaceted role in discipleship, teaching, guiding, and empowering believers to grow in the image of Christ. The Holy Spirit is God Himself, the third person of the Godhead, sent by the Father and the Son to dwell in believers and gifted to us by God the Father. The Holy Spirit keeps us connected to God the Father and Jesus Christ, seated at the right hand. The Bible reveals the Holy Spirit as our Advocate and Comforter who teaches, edifies, disciplines, and develops us for a deeper relationship with God.

The Powerful Work of the Holy Spirit in the Believer's Life

What He Does	Scripture Reference)	Brief Description
Guides the believer	Acts 8:29; Romans 8:14	Leads and directs in daily life and decisions.
Gives assurance of salvation	Romans 8:14–17	Confirms we are God's children and heirs with Christ.
Teaches the believer	1 John 2:27	It instructs us in God's truth and gives us understanding.
Intercedes for us	Romans 8:26	Prays on our behalf when we don't know how to pray.
Comforts	John 14:16	Brings peace and presence; never leaves us alone.
Sanctifies	2 Thessalonians 2:13	Works to make us holy and more like Christ.
Accomplishes regeneration	John 3:6	Brings about the new birth of spiritual life in Christ.
Reveals sin	John 16:8	Convicts us of sin and the need for repentance.
Reveals the truth of the Gospel	John 16:8, 13–14	Leads us to believe in Christ by revealing the truth.
Empowers us to witness	Acts 1:8; 4:31	Gives boldness and strength to share the gospel.
Destroys the power of sin	Romans 8:2–6	Sets us free from sin's control.
Leads and controls our lives	Romans 8:14; Galatians 5:16, 25	Directs our lives and enables us to walk in step with Him.
Distributes spiritual gifts	1 Corinthians 12:4–11	Equips believers with gifts for service and ministry.

In John 14:26 (KJV), But the Comforter, which is the Holy Ghost, whom the Father will send in my name, he shall teach you all things, and bring all things to your remembrance, whatsoever I have said unto you." This teaching role is foundational to discipleship because the Holy Spirit continually reminds us of the words of Jesus, who is the Word of God and the Bread of Life (John 1:1; John 6:35). He doesn't just give us head knowledge; He imparts truth in a way that transforms our hearts and renews our minds. The Holy Spirit instructs believers in God's truth and helps us navigate every decision, every challenge, and every season in alignment with the Word of God (the bread of life).

The Holy Spirit empowers believers for service and strengthens them to live in accordance with God's will. In Acts 1:8 (KJV), Jesus declares, "But ye shall receive power, after that the Holy Ghost comes upon you: and ye shall be witnesses unto me... unto the uttermost part of the earth." This empowerment equips Christians to witness the Gospel and fulfill God's mission boldly. Without the Holy Spirit, believers would lack the strength and wisdom to accomplish God's work or live lives worthy of their calling. Another significant role of the Holy Spirit in discipleship is His intercession in prayer. In Romans 8:26-27 (KJV), it is written, "Likewise the Spirit also helpeth our infirmities: for we know not what we should pray for as we ought: but the Spirit itself maketh intercession for us with groanings which cannot be uttered. And he that searcheth the hearts knoweth what is the mind of the Spirit, because he maketh intercession for the saints according to the will of God." When believers struggle to pray or understand God's will, the Holy Spirit intercedes, aligning their prayers with God's perfect purposes and drawing them closer to Him.

> A life style of prayer increases our intimacy with God and is what he uses to give us authority to usher our lives and the lives of those around us into his perfect will. The HS is the plug connected to the source (God & Christ), prayer is the cord that allows the power of the living God to flow.
>
> Danielle Thompson

Ultimately, the Holy Spirit transforms disciples into the image of Christ. As Romans 8:14 (KJV) reminds us, "For as many as are led by the Spirit of God, they are the sons of God." By yielding to the Holy Spirit, believers are led into all truth, empowered to live for Christ, and equipped to bear fruit. This Christ-like fruit is described in Galatians 5:22-23 (KJV): "But the fruit of the Spirit is love, joy, peace, longsuffering, gentleness, goodness, faith, meekness, temperance: against such there is no law."

In discipleship, the Holy Spirit's work is essential. He guides believers into truth, strengthens them for service, intercedes in their prayers, and produces spiritual fruit, enabling them to reflect the love and character of Christ in every aspect of their lives. Discipleship, therefore, is a continual process of yielding to the Holy Spirit's transforming power.

Chapter Eight: Obedience in the Process

At the core of obedience is a surrendered heart, a will yielded to God's voice, even when the request seems small or inconvenient. The apostle John wrote, "For this is the love of God, that we keep His commandments: and His commandments are not grievous" (1 John 5:3, KJV). Faithful obedience flows from love, love that recognizes who God is, trusts His character, and desires to please Him above all else. Jesus said, "If ye love me, keep my commandments" (John 14:15, KJV).

Our obedience is not simply about rule-keeping; it is our love answering His love. When we grasp how deeply God has loved us, even the smallest instruction becomes an opportunity to honor Him. Each "yes" to His voice draws us closer, deepens our trust, and makes His presence tangible in every part of our lives. To obey is to willingly yield to the guidance of the One who knows us best, our Heavenly Father.

In the original Greek, the word used for obedience is hypakoē (ὑπακοή, Strong's G5218), derived from hypakouō, meaning "to listen attentively, to hearken, to submit." It paints the picture of a heart that not only hears but responds with willing surrender. Faithful obedience, then, is not rooted in duty or fear, but in love. It is the ear turned toward heaven and the life aligned in response. Obedience begins in the quiet moments, those everyday decisions that shape our walk with God. Jesus said, "My sheep hear my voice, and I know them, and they follow me" (John 10:27, KJV). God continually speaks to His children, guiding, leading, and calling them into deeper fellowship. But the real question remains: Are we truly listening? And beyond hearing, are we willing to follow where he leads?

What does obedience look like in our day-to-day lives? Sometimes, it's as simple as hearing God say, "Go left" and turning left without hesitation. Sometimes, it's God whispering, "Get up and go to the kitchen" in the middle of your quiet time, and you get up and move because you trust that His promptings are leading you to something greater. Grand revelations don't always mark obedience; more often, it's found in small, consistent acts of faith that cultivate trust in God. It's worshiping as you walk through the supermarket, not waiting for a Sunday service or a worship night to encounter His presence. Worship is not bound by place or time; it's a posture of the heart, whether in solitude or among strangers. "Whatever you do [whatever your task may be], work from the soul [that is, put in your very best effort], as [something done] for the Lord and not for men, knowing [with all certainty] that it is from the Lord [not from men] that you will receive the inheritance which is your [greatest] reward. It is the Lord Christ whom you [actually] serve." (Colossians 3:23-24, AMP). **Every moment is an opportunity to obey and honor God.**

Obedience also manifests in our relationships. God may prompt you to release a friendship that hinders your growth or to reach out to someone you once dismissed. The challenge lies in obeying without hesitation. It can be difficult to yield when the request feels uncomfortable or contradicts what we want, but God's wisdom surpasses our own. "Trust in the Lord with all thine heart; and lean not unto thine own understanding. In all thy ways acknowledge him, and he shall direct thy paths" (Proverbs 3:5-6, KJV).

When God speaks, even about something that feels small or inconvenient, He leads you toward something greater. Obedience is not about the immediate gratification or transactional blessing, though blessings are never far from those who walk in His will. Sometimes, obedience means sitting out an event everyone expects you to attend or stepping back from the crowd to heed the Holy Spirit's whisper. "Be not conformed to this world: but be ye transformed by renewing your mind" (Romans 12:2, KJV). Choosing His voice over the pull of the world is a sacred act of devotion, and one act of obedience can alter the entire trajectory of your life or the lives of others.

There is power in immediate obedience. Delayed obedience is often rooted in doubt, fear, or a lack of reverence for God; however, when we obey God immediately, we demonstrate our trust in Him. Abraham modeled this when God told him to leave his home and go to a place he didn't know, which is one of the Bible's most powerful examples of obedience (Genesis 12:1-4). He didn't hesitate. He didn't ask questions. He yielded to God's will out of the intimate relationship he had with God, which led to the physical act of obedience. And through his obedience, God made him the father of many nations. When God calls us to act, we are stepping into His plan for our lives and the lives of others. When God says "go," you go. When he says "stop," you stop. When he says "pray," you pray. And in every act of obedience, His glory is revealed. "To obey is better than sacrifice" (1 Samuel 15:22, KJV).

Chapter Nine: The Weight of Who You Follow

Discipleship will always move you in one of two directions: toward spiritual growth or toward spiritual stagnation. The difference often lies in the spiritual health of the one guiding you. If a leader is walking closely with God, they can help you flourish in your faith. But when that same leader drifts into disobedience or worldly desires, they can unintentionally lead you into bondage, confusion, and spiritual decline. Jesus gave a clear warning: "Let them alone. They are blind leaders of the blind. And if the blind lead the blind, both will fall into a ditch" (Matthew 15:14, NKJV).

It's possible to be discipled by someone who once burned with passion for Christ, someone whose faith, love, and obedience helped you grow in one season. As time unfolds, you may watch that same person waver, compromising in areas they once guarded fiercely. That doesn't mean their faith was never genuine. It often means the enemy has found an open door through pride, sin, weariness, or subtle deception and begun to influence their heart, without their awareness. Watching this unfold can stir deep grief and disappointment, yet it also reminds us why discernment is essential for every believer.

Discernment is the God-given ability to understand deeply, evaluate carefully, and distinguish wisely so decisions align with truth and God's will. This word carries layers of meaning across the Hebrew and Greek texts.

- *Hebrew, Binah (Strongs, H998):* Refers to understanding and insight, the ability to perceive differences and grasp deeper meaning beyond surface knowledge.

- *Greek, Diakrisis (Strongs, G1253)* emphasizes distinguishing clearly between truth and error, particularly in spiritual and moral matters.
- *Greek, Dokimazō (Strong's, G1381):* Highlights discernment as an active process of testing and examining in order to approve what is genuine and sound.

Discernment is Holy Spirit-led perception; it is the insight from the Holy Spirit that enables us to recognize truth from imitation, light from shadow, a good thing from a God thing, and divine direction from human opinion. Discernment grows in intimacy with God. Without closeness to His voice, even the most well-meaning believer can mistake human influence for divine instruction.

Intimacy with God must remain your anchor. He may choose to feed you through a specific leader, ministry, or place for a season, but then call you to move in another direction. Trusting God allows you to let go when it's time. You need discernment to know when a season has ended and the courage to follow His leading. Without it, you risk being caught in the sifting of the enemy. You need the mind of Christ to discern by way of the Holy Spirit in order to obey (1 Corinthians 2:14-16, John 16:13 NKJV).

No matter who is leading you, the voice of the living God must remain your ultimate authority. Jesus said, "My sheep hear My voice, and I know them, and they follow Me" (John 10:27, NKJV). If God directs you one way and your leader directs you in a different direction, obedience to God must come first. Any leader who demands loyalty above obedience to the Lord is not safe to follow. If a leader lives in unrepentant sin, they can only lead you toward more sin and, ultimately, destruction.

Characteristics of Holy Spirit-Led Discipleship vs. Compromised Discipleship

Holy Spirit-Led Discipleship	Compromised Discipleship
Christ-Centered Discipleship that keeps Jesus at the center, focusing on His teachings and example. "I am the vine, you are the branches. He who abides in Me, and I in him, bears much fruit; for without Me you can do nothing." (John 15:5, NKJV)	**Elevates Leaders Above Christ** When leadership becomes the focus rather than Jesus, it leads to idolatry and misplaced loyalty. "For when one says, 'I am of Paul,' and another, 'I am of Apollos,' are you not carnal?" (1 Corinthians 3:4, NKJV)
Encourages Correction in Love Fosters accountability and growth through truth spoken in love. "Iron sharpens iron, so a man sharpens the countenance of his friend." (Proverbs 27:17, NKJV)	**Relies on Human Wisdom** Leans on tradition and opinion rather than the authority of God's Word. "Beware lest anyone cheat you through philosophy and empty deceit, according to the tradition of men." (Colossians 2:8, NKJV)
Grounded in Scripture Aligns all teaching and practice with the Word of God, encouraging obedience to His commands. "All Scripture is given by inspiration of God, and is profitable for doctrine, for reproof, for correction, for instruction in righteousness." (2 Timothy 3:16, NKJV)	**Uses Manipulation or Fear** Leads through control or fear, creating unhealthy dependency instead of spiritual maturity. "For God has not given us a spirit of fear, but of power and of love and of a sound mind." (2 Timothy 1:7, NKJV)
Equips Others for Service Empowers believers to grow in their callings and disciple others. "And He Himself gave some to be apostles, some prophets, some evangelists, and some pastors and teachers, for the equipping of the saints for the work of ministry." (Ephesians 4:11-12, NKJV)	**Avoids Accountability** Rejects correction and resists transparency, leading to unchecked sin. "The rod and rebuke give wisdom, but a child left to himself brings shame to his mother." (Proverbs 29:15, NKJV)
Focuses on Spiritual Transformation Prioritizes inward renewal through the Holy Spirit, producing fruit such as love, joy, peace, and self-control. "But the fruit of the Spirit is love, joy, peace, longsuffering, kindness, goodness, faithfulness, gentleness, self-control." (Galatians 5:22-23, NKJV)	**Lacks Christlike Compassion** Treats people as expendable or unworthy, failing to reflect Christ's example of love and servanthood.

Chapter Ten: Spiritual Growth and Maturity

Spiritual growth and maturity are essential in the life of a disciple of Christ. Just as a fisherman improves his craft with time and practice, so too does a disciple grow in faith through intentional effort, Spirit-led guidance, and godly leadership. A fisherman learns the patterns of the waves, the best times to cast his net, and the skill to draw in the catch. Likewise, we learn to discern God's timing, respond to His voice, and apply His Word in every season. Paul reminds us, "I planted, Apollos watered, but God gave the increase" (1 Corinthians 3:6, KJV).

Discipleship comes in many layers. Sometimes we plant seeds through a conversation, other times we water through consistent encouragement, prayer, or service, but it is always God who brings the growth. This can happen through words, but often it happens without them, as we witness through the way we live. "Love shall cover the multitude of sins" (1 Peter 4:8, KJV), and God expresses His love toward us in many "languages" through provision, acts of kindness, His spoken Word, moments of deep intimacy, and the sacrifice of Christ. In turn, we reflect His love through our own unique contributions. These contributions reveal both the fruits of the Holy Spirit and the gifts of the Holy Spirit.

Gifts of the Spirit (1 Corinthians 12:4–11)

Gift of the Spirit	What It Means	Purpose / How It Helps the Body
Word of Wisdom	Special insight to apply God's truth to situations.	Gives direction, clarity, and godly guidance.
Word of Knowledge	Supernatural understanding of facts or truths that you could not know naturally.	Reveals information needed for ministry or encouragement.
Faith	Extraordinary confidence in God's power and promises.	Strengthens others and activates bold trust in God.
Gifts of Healing	Supernatural ability to bring physical, emotional, or spiritual healing.	Demonstrates God's compassion and power.
Working of Miracles	Acts of power that go beyond natural laws.	Confirms God's presence and builds faith.
Prophecy	Speaking messages inspired by the Holy Spirit, encouragement, correction, or revelation.	Builds up, exhorts, and comforts the body (1 Cor. 14:3).
Discerning of Spirits	Ability to distinguish between the Holy Spirit, human spirits, and demonic influence.	Protects the body from deception.
Different Kinds of Tongues	Speaking in unknown, Spirit-inspired languages.	Encourages the believer and can benefit the body when
Interpretation of Tongues	Understanding and communicating the meaning of tongues.	Allows tongues to edify and instruct the whole body.

Fruit of the Holy Spirit (Galatians 5:22–23)

Fruit of the Spirit	Simple Definition	How It Shows Up in Life
Love	Selfless, unconditional care and compassion.	Being patient, forgiving, and putting others' needs before your own.
Joy	Deep, God-given gladness not based on circumstances.	Staying positive and thankful, even in difficult times.
Peace	Inner calm and trust in God.	Remaining steady, not anxious or easily shaken.
Long-suffering (Patience)	Ability to endure hardship or delay without anger.	Responding gently instead of reacting quickly.
Kindness	Being considerate, gentle, and thoughtful.	Treating others with warmth and compassion.
Goodness	Moral integrity: doing what is right.	Making choices that honor God and bless people.
Faithfulness	Loyalty, commitment, and dependability.	Keeping promises; being trustworthy and consistent.
Gentleness	Strength under control; humility and meekness.	Responding softly, not harshly; treating others with respect.
Self-Control	Discipline over desires, emotions, and actions.	Saying "no" to impulses; choosing what is wise instead of what is easy.

The gifts of the Spirit are all tools in the hands of a faithful fisherman, each used to draw souls into the safety of His net. The goal is always the same: to align our hearts with His and let every action, word, and motive point others to Him.

And the way we know if we are truly growing in Christ is by examining the kind of fruit our lives are producing. The Bible says, "You will know them by their fruits. Do men gather grapes from thornbushes or figs from thistles?"(Matthew 7:16, NKJV). As disciples, we must pause and examine the fruit of our lives. Are we growing in the attributes that reflect the Spirit of God?

- Are you more patient, kind, loving, and gentle?
- Do you wait on the Lord well and endure trials with faith?
- Do you extend love and forgiveness even when others hurt you?

Or are you falling back into old patterns using things like drugs, alcohol, sex, or unhealthy relationships to cope with frustration? Are you angry at others instead of turning to God for peace? The fruit of our lives is a reflection of the God we serve. Paul reminds us in Galatians 5:22-23 (NKJV): But the fruit of the Spirit is love, joy, peace, long-suffering, kindness, goodness, faithfulness, gentleness, self-control. Against such, there is no law." While none of us are perfect, as the Word reminds us, "for all have sinned and fall short of the glory of God" (Romans 3:23, NKJV), we should still strive daily to live a life that bears good fruit and glorifies God. "But as He who called you is holy, you also be holy in all your conduct" (1 Peter 1:15, NKJV).

Spiritual growth begins with the Word of God. "As newborn babes, desire the pure milk of the word, that you may grow thereby" (1 Peter 2:2, NKJV). You cannot grow without God's Word; it is living, breathing, and active. As Hebrews 4:12 (NKJV) declares: "For the word of God is living and powerful, and sharper than any two-edged sword, piercing even to the division of soul and spirit, and of joints and marrow, and is a discerner of the thoughts and intents of the heart."

Take these steps to strengthen your spiritual life

1. Know and Live the Word: "Your word I have hidden in my heart, that I might not sin against You" (Psalm 119:11, NKJV). It is not enough to simply read the Word; you must live it. Allow it to guide your actions, transform your mind, and renew your heart.
2. Rely on the Holy Spirit. The Holy Spirit is your Teacher and Guide. Jesus said, "But the Helper, the Holy Spirit, whom the Father will send in My name, He will teach you all things, and bring to your remembrance all things that I said to you" (John 14:26, NKJV). Invite the Holy Spirit to disciple you, convict you of sin, and help you bear the fruit of righteousness.
3. Seek Godly Leadership. Good leadership is vital to spiritual growth. Surround yourself with leaders and mentors who are Christ-centered, grounded in Scripture, and whose lives bear the fruit of the Spirit. "Imitate me, just as I also imitate Christ" (1 Corinthians 11:1, NKJV).
4. Practice Holiness Daily Strive to be holy, not by your strength but through God's grace and the power of the Holy Spirit. "Therefore, having these promises, beloved, let us cleanse ourselves from all filthiness of the flesh and spirit, perfecting holiness in the fear of God" (2 Corinthians 7:1, NKJV).
5. Endure Trials with Faith: Trials are part of spiritual growth. James encourages us, "My brethren, count it all joy when you fall into various trials, knowing that the testing of your faith produces patience. But let patience have its perfect work, that you may be perfect and complete, lacking nothing" (James 1:2-4, NKJV).

Spiritual growth is not about perfection, but about striving to be more like Christ every day. Take up your cross, die to your flesh, and live by the Spirit. As Paul reminds us, "I press toward the goal for the prize of the upward call of God in Christ Jesus" (Philippians 3:14, NKJV). Your spiritual growth depends on your relationship with God, commitment to His Word, and reliance on the Holy Spirit. Let your life bear witness to God the Father, for His transformative Word is not separate from Him; God is His Word, and through it, He reveals His character, personality, and expectations.

Chapter Eleven: Evangelism and Discipleship

Evangelism and discipleship work hand in hand to fulfill the Great Commission. To reach others for Christ, you must first draw them in, just like a fisherman uses bait to catch fish. The difference is that we use the love of God. Jesus said, "Follow Me, and I will make you fishers of men"(Matthew 4:19, NKJV). Without the "bait" of evangelism, sharing the good news of Jesus, you cannot make disciples.

Evangelism is casting the net. It shares the message of salvation and points people to Jesus. The Samaritan woman at the well is a perfect example. After encountering Jesus, she ran back to her village saying, "Come, see a Man who told me all things that I ever did. Could this be the Christ?" (John 4:29, NKJV). Her testimony drew others to Him. Many believed not because of her title, position, or authority but because she openly shared what Jesus had done for her. Evangelism, then, is not merely about words; it is the visible evidence of God's work in your life. Psalm 34:8 (KJV) extends this same invitation: "O taste and see that the Lord is good: blessed is the man that trusteth in Him." When others see the joy, peace, and transformation that God has worked in you, they are drawn to that same hope. Evangelism (net casting) spreads the seed through your testimony, devotion, and the light of Christ shining through you.

The discipleship journey continuously waters the seeds planted. It is the intentional process of walking with others as they grow in their faith, teaching, mentoring, and helping them live out the Word of God. Jesus commanded, "Go therefore and make disciples of all the nations, baptizing them in the name of the Father and of the Son and of the Holy Spirit, teaching them to observe all things that I have commanded you" (Matthew 28:19-20, NKJV). Discipleship is a collaborative process. God may call you to share the message with many, but to disciple only a few. Sometimes the Holy Spirit assigns you only to plant the seed. Other times, you may be called to water it. Still, it is always God who makes it grow. That is why intimacy with the Holy Spirit is vital. Discipleship is not about control but collaboration. Evangelism illuminates the light of Christ in you, and discipleship deepens that relationship into maturity. Both are necessary. Both are part of the mission. Your testimony and your life are living invitations to encounter Jesus. "Let your light shine before men, that they may see your good works and glorify your Father in heaven" (Matthew 5:16, NKJV). Together, evangelism and discipleship are inseparable parts of the gospel mission.

This call is not only for pastors and missionaries, but also for all who belong to Christ. The question is: are you making yourself available? Will you plant when He says plant? Water when He says water? And rejoice when God brings the harvest? When He is lifted up in your words, your actions, and your love, He will draw all people to Himself (John 12:32, NKJV).

Let your life be a tool in the hands of the Master, bold in evangelism, faithful in discipleship, and surrendered to the Holy Spirit who empowers you to make an eternal impact.

To be a fisher of men is not only to preach but to live in such a way that Christ is seen in you. It is obeying God when He says open your home to the hurting, listening with compassion, sharing the gospel at a coffee shop, mentoring a new believer, or simply showing consistent love in your workplace. Discipleship is both spoken and demonstrated. Jesus modeled this for us: He served, loved, forgave, and sacrificed. He didn't just teach discipleship; He embodied it. And the beautiful truth is, we are never alone in this work. Jesus closes the Great Commission with a promise: "Lo, I am with you always, even unto the end of the world." (Matthew 28:20, KJV). The Holy Spirit is your power, your comfort, and your guide. He equips you with boldness, wisdom, and endurance to fulfill this calling.

As we end this journey, remember that discipleship begins with intimacy with Jesus. When you walk with Him daily, your life becomes the message, your love becomes the net, and your obedience becomes the testimony. The Great Commission is not just a command but an invitation to partner with Christ in bringing His kingdom to earth.

So rise up, disciple of Jesus. Live surrendered, love deeply, and lead others to the One who gave His life for all. The harvest is plentiful, the call is clear, and His presence is with you always.

<u>The waters are ready, the nets are in your hands, now go fish for men.</u>

What Really is A Fisher of Men

Key Terms	Definitions Based on scriptural themes, paraphrased
Discipleship	The ongoing process of spiritual transformation becoming more like Christ in heart, character, and action through daily relationship, obedience, and learning from Jesus. (Luke 9:23; Romans 12:2) Strong's Concordance: • μαθητεύω (mathēteuō, G3100) – to train, teach, make a disciple. • μαθητής (mathētēs, G3101) – a learner, follower, pupil
Evangelism	The act of proclaiming the good news of Jesus Christ, His salvation, grace, and truth, inviting others into the Kingdom of God. (Matthew 28:19–20; Mark 16:15) Strong's Concordance: • εὐαγγελίζω (euangelizō, G2097) – to announce good news • εὐαγγέλιον (euangelion, G2098) – the gospel, glad tidings
Fisher of Men	A metaphor describing believers who draw others into God's Kingdom through Spirit-led witness and truth. (Matthew 4:19) Strong's Concordance: • ἁλιεύς (halieus, G231) – fisherman • ζωγρέω (zōgreō, G2221) – to capture alive
Obedience	A loving response of surrender and alignment to God's will, flowing from trust rather than obligation. (John 14:15; 1 Samuel 15:22) Strong's Concordance: • ὑπακοή (hypakoē, G5218) –

		attentive listening, submission
Discernment	The spiritual ability to distinguish truth from deception and perceive rightly by the Holy Spirit. (1 Corinthians 2:14–16; Hebrews 5:14) Strong's Concordance: <ul><li>בִּינָה (Binah, H998) – understanding, insight</li><li>διάκρισις (diakrisis, G1253) – discernment, distinguishing</li><li>δοκιμάζω (dokimazō, G1381) – to test and approve</li></ul>	
The Holy Spirit (Holy Ghost)	The third Person of the Trinity, dwelling within believers to guide, teach, convict, empower, and transform. (John 14:26; John 16:13) Strong's Concordance: <ul><li>πνεῦμα ἅγιον (pneuma hagion, G4151 / G40) – Holy Spirit</li></ul>	
Transformation	The inner renewal of heart and mind that reshapes believers into Christ's likeness by the Spirit's work. (Romans 12:2; 2 Corinthians 3:18) Strong's Concordance: <ul><li>μεταμορφόω (metamorphoō, G3339) – to transform, change form</li></ul>	
The Great Commission	Jesus' command to make disciples of all nations through going, baptizing, and teaching obedience to Him. (Matthew 28:18–20) Strong's Concordance: <ul><li>ἐξουσία (exousia, G1849) – authority</li><li>ἀποστέλλω (apostellō, G649) – to</li></ul>	

		send with authority
Spiritual Warfare		The spiritual conflict between God's Kingdom and darkness, fought through faith, prayer, and God's Word. (Ephesians 6:10–18; 2 Corinthians 10:4–5) Strong's Concordance: • πάλη (palē, G3823) – struggle, conflict • στρατεύομαι (strateuomai, G4754) – to wage war
Faithfulness		Steadfast loyalty to God and perseverance in His will, regardless of circumstances. (Galatians 6:9; Hebrews 11:1) Strong's Concordance: • πιστός (pistos, G4103) – faithful, trustworthy
Fruit of the Spirit		The visible evidence of the Holy Spirit's character manifested in a believer's life. (Galatians 5:22–23) Strong's Concordance: • καρπός (karpos, G2590) – fruit, outcome
Surrender		A complete yielding of one's will, desires, and control to God's authority. (Luke 22:42; James 4:7) Strong's Concordance: • ὑποτάσσω (hypotassō, G5293) – to submit, place under authority
Calling		God's divine invitation to fulfill His purpose, both universal and personal, in the believer's life. (Romans 8:28–30; John 15:16) Strong's Concordance: • καλέω (kaleō, G2564) – to call, invite

The Word of God	God's living truth revealed through Scripture and fully embodied in Jesus Christ. (John 1:1; 2 Timothy 3:16–17) Strong's Concordance: • λόγος (logos, G3056) – word, divine expression
Kingdom of God	God's sovereign rule and reign, present wherever His will is obeyed and fully realized in eternity. (Luke 17:20–21; Matthew 6:33) Strong's Concordance: • βασιλεία (basileia, G932) – kingdom, reign
Abide	To remain continually connected to Christ as the source of spiritual life and fruitfulness. (John 15:4–5) Strong's Concordance: • μένω (menō, G3306) – to remain, dwell
Anointing	The Holy Spirit's empowering presence that equips believers to accomplish God's purposes. (1 John 2:27) Strong's Concordance: • χρίσμα (chrisma, G5545) – anointing
Authority	Divine right and power given by Christ to advance God's Kingdom and overcome darkness. (Luke 10:19) Strong's Concordance: • ἐξουσία (exousia, G1849) – authority, delegated power

Brokenness	A posture of humility where self-reliance is surrendered, and God's strength is revealed. (Psalm 51:17) Strong's Concordance: • דָּכָא (daka, H1792) – crushed, humbled
Covenant	A sacred, binding agreement initiated by God, fulfilled through Jesus Christ. (Luke 22:20) Strong's Concordance: • בְּרִית (berith, H1285) – covenant • διαθήκη (diathēkē, G1242) – covenant, testament
Grace	God's unearned favor and empowering presence that transforms and sustains believers. (2 Corinthians 12:9) Strong's Concordance: • χάρις (charis, G5485) – grace, favor
Harvest	The gathering of souls into God's Kingdom through faithful gospel labor. (Matthew 9:37) Strong's Concordance: • θερισμός (therismos, G2326) – harvest
Humility	A heart posture of dependence on God that opens the door to grace and wisdom. (James 4:6) Strong's Concordance: • ταπεινόω (tapeinoō, G5013) – to humble
Intercession	Standing in prayer on behalf of others, aligning with God's heart and will. (Hebrews 7:25) Strong's Concordance: • ἐντυγχάνω (entynchano, G1793) –

		to intercede
Kingdom Mindset	A worldview shaped by God's eternal priorities rather than earthly systems. (Matthew 6:33) Strong's Concordance: • φρόνημα (phronēma, G5427) – mindset, way of thinking	
Renewal	Spiritual restoration and refreshing of the mind and inner life by the Holy Spirit. (Ephesians 4:23) Strong's Concordance: • ἀνακαινόω (anakainoō, G341) – to renew	
Repentance	A decisive turning from sin toward God that results in transformed living. (Matthew 4:17) Strong's Concordance: • μετάνοια (metanoia, G3341) – change of mind and direction	
Sanctification	The ongoing process of being set apart and made holy for God's purposes. (1 Thessalonians 4:3) Strong's Concordance: • ἁγιασμός (hagiasmos, G38) – holiness, consecration	
Stewardship	Faithful management of what God entrusts for His glory and Kingdom advancement. (1 Corinthians 4:2) Strong's Concordance: • οἰκονόμος (oikonomos, G3623) – steward, manager	

Submission	Willing alignment under God's authority and trust in His wisdom. (James 4:7) Strong's Concordance: • ὑποτάσσω (hypotassō, G5293) – to submit
Trust	Confident reliance on God's character, promises, and faithfulness. (Proverbs 3:5) Strong's Concordance: • בָּטַח (batach, H982) – to trust, rely
Yielding	Daily surrender to the Holy Spirit's leadership and direction. (Galatians 5:16) Strong's Concordance: • παρίστημι (paristēmi, G3936) – to present, yield

About Jhinelle Thompson

Jhinelle Thompson is a professor, creative educator, and above all, a devoted child of God with over a decade of experience in the education field. She is a woman of faith who seeks God's heart and leads through the guidance of the Holy Spirit in every area of her life and work.

Jhinelle is a transformative leader who inspires growth and drives meaningful change in individuals and organizations. God has gifted her with a deep passion to teach and equip people to pursue God's heart and to make disciples who reflect His character. Her mission is to educate, equip, and empower others to draw closer to God, grow in spiritual maturity, and walk boldly in radical obedience.

www.ingramcontent.com/pod-product-compliance
Lightning Source LLC
Chambersburg PA
CBHW031422160426
43196CB00008B/1020